AF231244

Thank You, Mr. Jenkins

Written by Darin Sargent
Adapted and Illustrated by Josh Zamora

ISBN 13: 978-0-9820141-3-4
ISBN 10: 0-9820141-3-9

Published by Darin Sargent and Josh Zamora.

Produced in 2009 in the United States of America
as a service of Simple Publishing,
a divison of Woolstrum Publishing House, LLC.

www.simple-publishing.com

Printed in the United States of America
on acid-free paper.

16 15 14 13 12 11 10 09 08 07 06 05 04 03 02 01

DARIN

To the love of my life, Duana: You have always believed in me – I love you with my whole heart.

To Carson, Ashton, + Averie: Being your dad is the greatest joy of my life! Thanks for your input on the book. You helped me see it through kids eyes.

You guys ROCK!!

To Mom + Dad: Before Nike ever said it, it was our mantra – JUST DO IT!!

Thanks for never giving up on me.

To Josh: You are one of a kind!! Thanks for inspiring this project and for believing in me and this book! I am forever in your debt. You are more than an illustrator – You are a true friend.

And of course to Mr. Jenkins: YOU CHANGED MY LIFE!! This book says it all.

JOSH

To my awesome wife Narissa: Thank you for your love. I love you so much and couldn't be prouder to be your husband.

To Noah: You're such a great little boy. I love you, and I'm so proud of you!!!

To Darin: Inspirational! Thanks for the motivation and the constant reminders that we can actually make a difference.

To Mom + Dad + the rest of my familia: Thank you guys so much. I love you!

To all of the teachers in my life: See? All of the constant doodling was worth it. Even if I got in trouble for it sometimes.

Dedicated to all of the "Mr. Jenkins" out there.

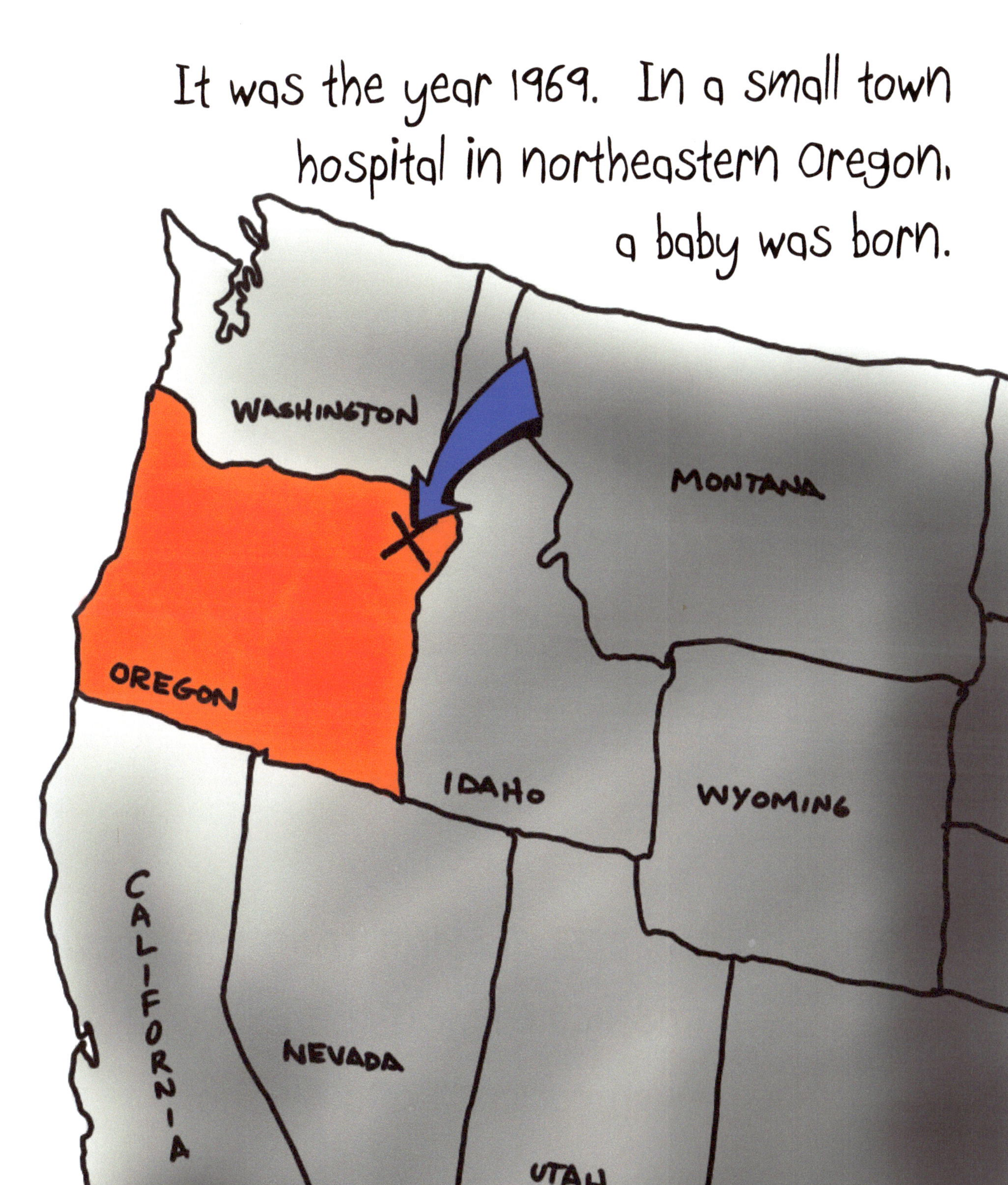

It was the year 1969. In a small town hospital in northeastern Oregon, a baby was born.
WASHINGTON
MONTANA
OREGON
IDAHO
WYOMING
CALIFORNIA
NEVADA
UTAH

Born with one arm missing from the elbow down.
I was immediately the cause of
much concern and emotion.

Like most births, this one was long expected and hopeful. The husband and wife were so very excited to have a brand new baby in their lives.

But I was loved from day one.
Even though I was different, I was loved.

As I grew older,
I quickly learned that there were some
things that were very difficult
for me to do.

Tying my shoes was tough
and shuffling cards was impossible.

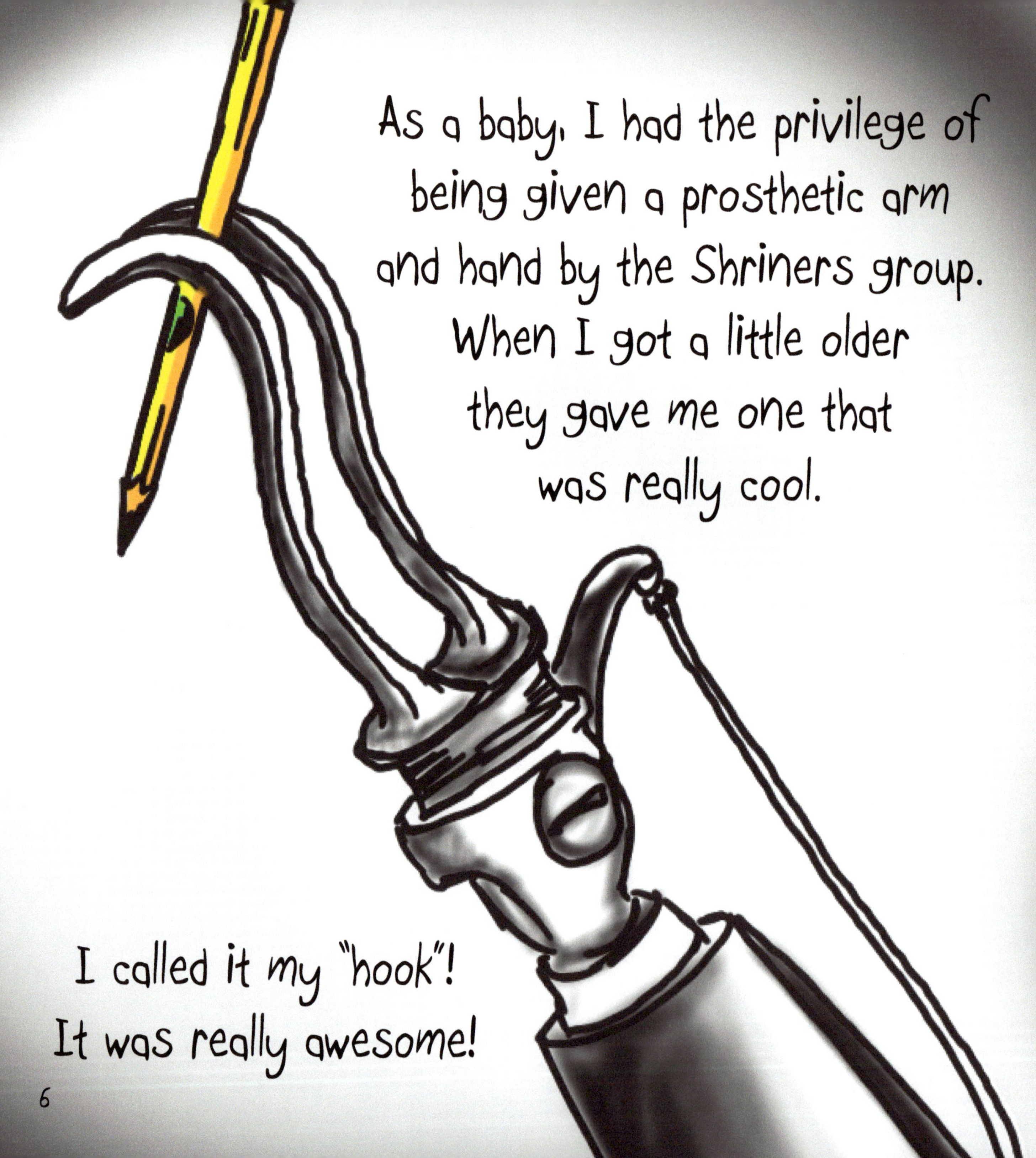

As a baby, I had the privilege of being given a prosthetic arm and hand by the Shriners group. When I got a little older they gave me one that was really cool.

I called it my "hook"!
It was really awesome!

My hook helped me out a lot.

I could grab things with it
and use it almost like a
normal extension of my body.

My parents never forced me to wear it,
so I really got to appreciate having it.

It became very "handy" for all sorts of
activities.

First
Grade

I was so excited about getting into first grade.

FIRST GRADE!!! Where the boys were mean and the girls were icky. You know, THAT GRADE.

I was still fairly new to this
I-only-have-one-arm-thingamajig,
so I wasn't prepared for what was in store for me. I had decided to wear my hook to school that day, and I was looking forward to showing it to my friends.

BIG MISTAKE.

I quickly discovered that
I was really good at sports
and that I was fast,
super fast!

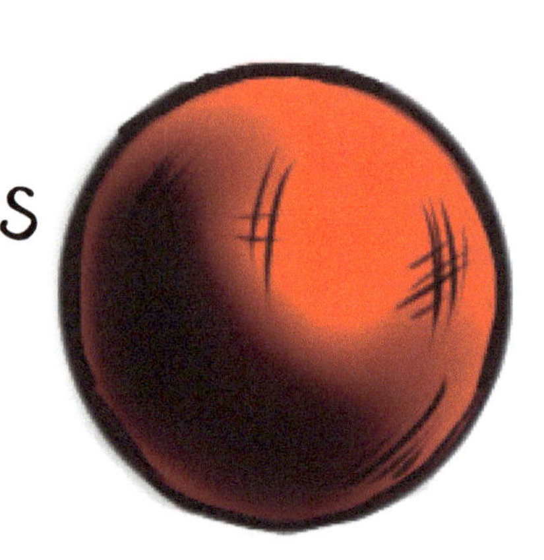

My hook was just an extension of my arm,
and I could do a lot with it. But that day, I found
out that I had to be
really careful with it;
it could be dangerous.
Going up for that ball
my friend and I were
playing with. I was a
little too fast for my
friend, and my hook

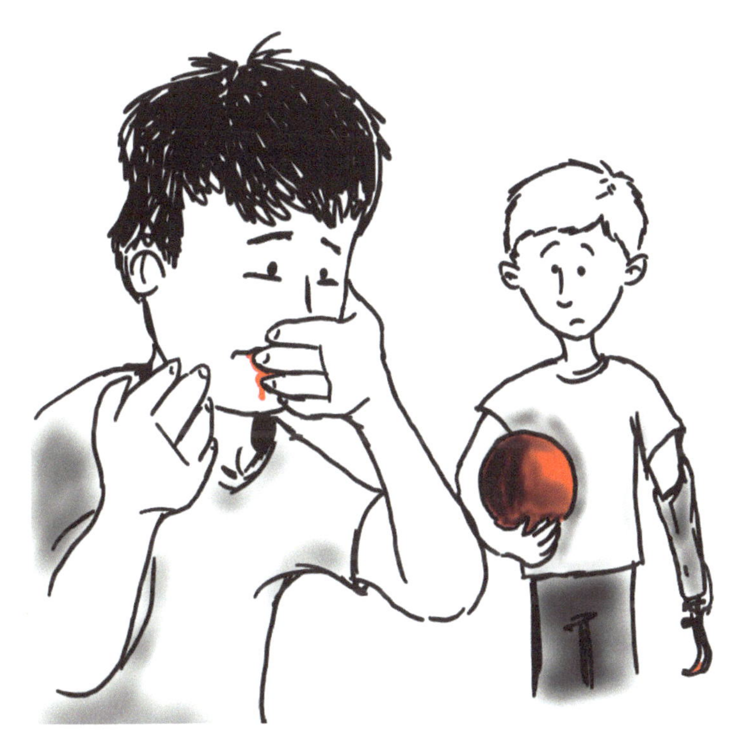

accidently punched through his lip. It was scary.
At 6 years old, that type of event was shocking
and unforgettable.

When recess was over, my teacher called me out of the classroom.

She never told me why she was mad at me.

Instead, she just began to yell at me, telling me that I was different than the other kids and that I wasn't allowed to wear my hook to school.

She told me that I had no right to be hurting the other kids (as if I had been trying to).

I will never forget the way my first grade teacher talked to me that day.

My heart was crushed.

I went home after school and told my parents
what had happened. My dad picked me up and put
me on his knee and told me,

"Son, you are not a mistake and you are no
different than anyone else. This is the way that
you were created. Don't ever let anyone
tell you any different."

14

Three years later we moved to a new state right in the middle of my 4th grade year.

I really wanted to fit in and be accepted and make new friends but being different made that almost impossible.

One day all the boys were playing football at recess. I wanted to play really bad and show them how I could win the game single-handedly.

But no one would let me play.

I was so bummed! I went and found my brother who was in the first grade. No one wanted to play with him, either. After all, he was the brother of the school's only one-armed kid.

Mr.
Jenkins
4th Grade

When the bell rang, I ventured back to my classroom, where I collapsed on my desk and began to sob like a baby. Everyone knows how difficult it is having to face the challenges of a new school and making new friends. It's tough enough for "normal" people, but for those of us who look different it's much harder.

I was miserable.

Mr. Jenkins was my 4th grade teacher. He saw that I wasn't doing too well, so he asked someone what had happened.

When he found out that I was having trouble fitting in, he gathered a small group of kids in front of the class.

He pointed out the differences between all of them, and then called me up. "Darin is just different, just like all of us are. We were all created unique"

Because of what Mr. Jenkins did that day, I was finally accepted for who I was.

From that day forward, everything changed for me.
I went on into Jr. High, and then into High School,
totally accepted for who I was.

I don't know where he is now. I'm not even sure
if he's alive, but if you are out there,
Mr. Jenkins, I have to say one thing:

Thank you!

I will never forget you for as long as I live.
You made a difference in my life!